McGillicutty

A Very Special Bear!

Priscilla Miller

Written by Priscilla Miller
Illustrated by Mary Guntzviller

Partial proceeds donated to foster children's charities

*Dedicated to all the special people who encouraged me to keep the promise
I made to my son Paul, so many years ago, that "someday" I would write a
story about McGillicutty, his very special bear.*

Published by Priscilla of Alden Publishing Co., P.O. Box 125, Alden, MI 49612. Telephone 231.331.5109. E-mail: priscilla@chartermi.net

Publisher's Cataloging-in-Publication Data
Miller, Priscilla
McGillicutty: a very special bear!/Priscilla Miller
Alden, Mich.
p.   cm.   ill.
ISBN 978-1-4951-3357-2
1. Children's Literature–United States.

PROJECT COORDINATION BY BOOKABILITY OF MICHIGAN LLC

Printed in Canada

One day, at the Whoops - a - Daisy Bear Factory,
things were moving along quite satisfactorily.

Mr. Whoops was finishing up one last little bear,
when his nose had a tickle from the dust in the air.

As he was putting a nose on that bear, he sneezed!
When he saw what had happened, he was not at all pleased.
As he went Ah-Ah-Chooo, his hand did shake,
causing him to make a mistake!

The face on that bear was something to see,
for the nose ended up where the mouth was to be.

"I can't fix his nose, I don't have any more!
I'll just have to send him off to the store!"

Cute little bears, each wearing a satin bow,
sitting on the store's shelf, all in a row.

People would stop, point their fingers, and stare.
"Look! Look! At that funny little bear!"
"Look at his chin! His nose is down there!"
"He's sure not a very cute-looking bear!"

Soon all the bears were sold, but that one, when a lady said, "I need a bear for my grandson. Today is his Birthday, and I just got off work!"

"This is the only one I have left," said the clerk.

Glossary Airship to Zeppelin

Airship: A balloon or envelope filled with a lighter-than-air gas, which gives it lift. It is powered by motors and steered by control surfaces or fins; it usually houses a gondola or cabin underneath. Airship is another name for skyship.

Altimeter: An instrument used by the pilot to determine the height of the airship above sea level. It senses changes in atmospheric pressure as the airship ascends and descends and registers these as changes in altitude.

Ballast: Everything on or inside the airship, including the helium and the air in the ballonets. "Disposable ballast" takes the form of water or shotbags. Dropping disposable ballast enables an airship to ascend or to compensate for helium loss or an increased payload.

Blimp: An airship that has no internal framework to maintain the shape of the envelope. Blimps are also called non-rigid, or pressure airships.

Buoyancy: The force that allows an airship to float in the air. This force comes from the air surrounding the airship in exactly the same way as buoyancy comes from the water surrounding a boat or submarine. The amount of buoyant force depends upon how much outside air the airship pushes aside or displaces. The bigger the airship, the greater the buoyant force.

Cables: Long steel ropes used to activate valves or control surfaces from the cockpit.

Center of Buoyancy: The center of the volume of the air that is displaced by the airship's envelope. Since the shape of the envelope cannot be changed, the location of the center of buoyancy cannot be changed.

Center of Gravity (CG): The point inside the airship where its entire weight is said to be concentrated. On Henry's skyship, the center of gravity is located a short distance above the gondola and in between the forward and rear ballonets. The entire airship is just like a see-saw hinged at this point.

Dirigible: Another word for "airship." It comes from the French "dirigeable," which means steerable or capable of being directed or guided.

Dynamic Lift: The aerodynamic lift generated by flying an airship with its nose up to compensate for heaviness or with its nose down to compensate for lightness.

Elevators: The moveable surfaces attached to an airship's horizontal tail fins used to control nose up and nose down movement.

Envelope: The gasbag, or hull, of a non-rigid airship.

Equilibrium: When the weight of the airship and its contents equals the weight of the outside air displaced by the envelope. In this condition, the airship's weight is zero.

Exposure: Flights over cities and towns so that large numbers of people can see the airship.

Fins: The fixed vertical and horizontal stabilizing surfaces attached to an airship's tail.

Gondola: The part of the airship that carries the pilots, passengers, payload, cabin and engines. It is always located on the bottom of the airship.

Gross Lift: The gross lift is equal to the total buoyant force acting on the airship minus the weight of the gasses inside the airship.

Helium: An odorless and non-flammable gas; it is the second lightest element known. Helium is used to inflate the fabric envelope, creating a light but strong structure.

Kevlar: A composite material used in the production of both the cables and gondola of an airship.

Landing Gear: The wheel-based mechanism below the gondola upon which the airship pivots and lands.

THE END

The lady said, "It will just have to do,
it's one o'clock and the party's at two!
Please wrap it up and put on a bow,
I'm in a hurry! I really must go!"

They sang "Happy Birthday", ate ice cream and cake.

As the lady thought, "Did I make a mistake?
If I had more time, I could have knitted a sweater!
Maybe a toy bunny would have been better."

Brightly wrapped gifts, all stacked in a pile,
"time to open them up!" he said, with a smile.

There were toy cars and trucks, even a bicycle to ride.

Then he tore open the box, with the bear inside.

He laughed as he said, "he's cute as can be!
He's not like any other bear, was he made just for me?"

"Yes, indeed!" said his Grandma, "he was made just for you!
An ordinary bear would just never do!"

Now an unusual name is what he chose,
for his little friend with the funny nose.
The little bear, his new best buddy,
Was given the name of McGillicutty!

While riding his bike, or in the tree house so high,
the boy always kept that bear nearby.

Each night at bedtime, he took his bear to bed,
wrapped his arms around it, and this is what he said.

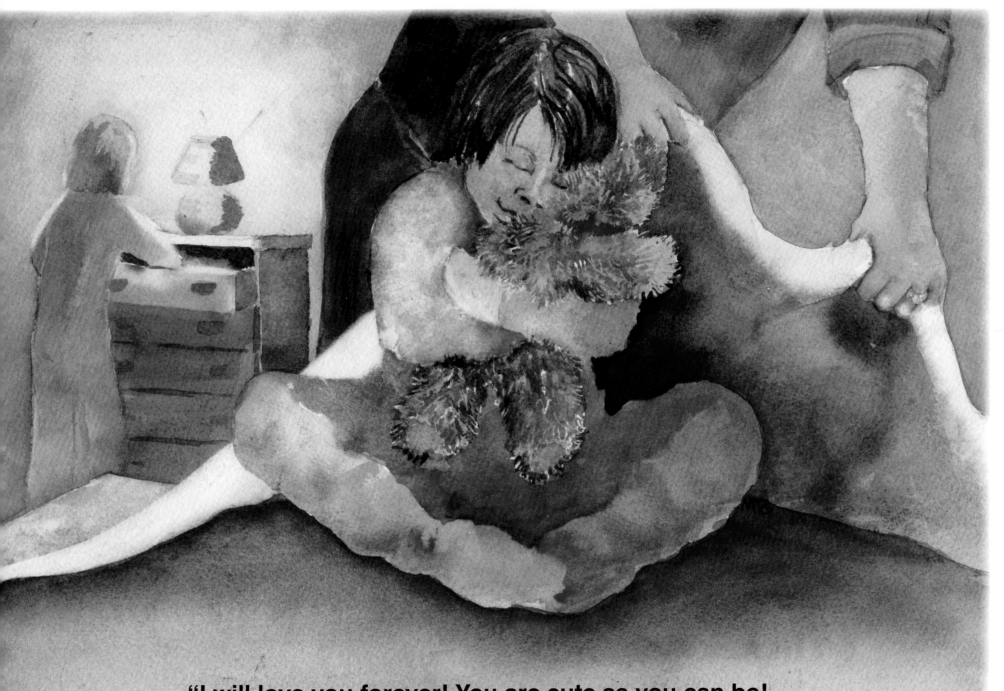

"I will love you forever! You are cute as you can be!
You're my own special bear, because you were made just for me!"

When Mom and Dad kissed him and tucked him in tight.
They heard him whisper, "McGillicutty, Good Night!"

About Author Priscilla Miller

The publication of *McGillicutty: A Very Special Bear* fulfills a promise Miller made to her young son over 40 years ago that "someday" she would write a story about his unusual looking bear, "McGillicutty."

Priscilla has lived in Michigan her entire life. She is a mother, grandmother and great grandmother. For the past twelve years, she and her husband Bill have made their home in Alden. Shortly after moving to northern Michigan, her first newspaper article was featured in the Father's Day Edition of the *Traverse City Record Eagle*. Despite receiving a diagnosis of Wet AMD (the leading cause of blindness in people over the age of 50), monthly eye treatments have slowed the progression of the disease. She continued to write for local newspapers, published a book, *Reflections at the Water's Edge: An Illustrated History of the Alden Area*, and has had three stories published in *Chicken Soup for the Soul* books.

In 2008, TV 7& 4 named her their "Hometown Hero" for spearheading a fundraiser for a baby needing a triple organ transplant. She served in a volunteer capacity as Antrim County High Tea for Breast Cancer Prevention's Publicity Chairman for four years. Since 2009, has organized Alden's Memorial Day Parade.

About Artist Mary Guntzviller

Guntzviller has a Bachelor of Fine Arts degree from Wayne State University, with a major in Art, including an emphasis in figure drawing and sculpture. She has been a professional artist since 1988.

The book, *Art of the Sleeping Bear Dunes: Transforming Nature into Art,* includes Guntzviller's painting, "Where Herons Play, Crystal River, Glen Arbor." This Plein-Air watercolor painting won first place in the Glen Arbor Paint-out in August 2012. The Dennos Museum, Traverse City, hosted the show which included all the paintings in the book and hung from October 13, 2013 – January 5, 2014.

In September, 2013, Guntzviller took second place at the Plein-Air paint out sponsored by the Artcenter Traverse City and the Botanical Garden Society of Northwest Michigan.

The Michigan Watercolor Society again accepted one of Guntzviller's paintings for their 2012 annual show in Saginaw. She has had paintings accepted three times by this prestigious watercolor society. Her "First Poppies" painting hung at the Detroit Institute of Arts, Detroit, MI, for their 50th anniversary traveling show.

Through both teaching and demonstrations, Guntzviller enthusiastically shares her work first-hand with others. Holding classes & workshops in watercolor, acrylics, and life drawing throughout the year, she teaches students confidence first, then composition, drawing skills and painting techniques. Teaching since 1993, she welcomes beginners and more experienced students. By appointment, she critiques paintings at her Studio in Bellaire, MI. A few of her workshop locations have been at St. John, Virgin Islands; Cincinnati, Ohio; Mackinac Island, MI; at the nationally known Artcenter, Traverse City, MI; and twice a year at the Road Scholar Kettering Center in Tustin, MI.

For Additional Copies

Contact Author Priscilla Miller
priscilla@chartermi.net
P.O. Box 125, Alden, MI 49612

$18.95 Each + $4.50 S & H

Volume Discounts Available

Partial Proceeds Donated to Benefit Foster Children

Environmental Benefit Statement

This book was manufactured using eco-friendly materials, including Friesen's Envirolux paper made with 80% recycled fiber and 60% post consumer waste to protect ancient forests and our environment.

		Eco-Friendly Materials		
Paper:	**Cover Board:**	**Inks:**	**Adhesives:**	**Waste:**
• Eco-friendly - Text - Cover	• Recycled • 100% Post Consumer Waste	• Vegetable based	• Water based • Renewable • Recyclable	• 100% Recycled

		Saved Resources		
Trees:	**Water:**	**Energy:**	**Greenhouse Gases:**	**Solid Waste:**
2 fully grown	1,599 gallons	2 million BTU's	295 pounds	107 pounds

Friesens pioneers eco-friendly history books.
Calculation based on research by Environmental Defense and other members of the paper task force.

 PROTECTS ANCIENT FORESTS

 **Friesens**

 RENEWABLE WATER-GENERATED POWER